Wonders of the Seasons

Written by Keith Brandt
Illustrated by James Watling

Troll Associates

Library of Congress Cataloging in Publication Data

Brandt, Keith
  Wonders of the seasons.

  Summary: Explains how the Earth's journey around
the sun creates our change of seasons.
    1. Seasons—Juvenile literature. [1. Seasons]
I. Watling, James. II. Title.
QB631.B68   574   81-7411
ISBN 0-89375-580-X   AACR2
ISBN 0-89375-581-8 (pbk.)

Snow is on the ground. Tree branches are bare. Days are short, nights are long. It is winter.

4

Soon the days grow longer. Tiny green buds appear on tree branches. Yellow daffodils and red tulips burst into bloom. New shoots of grass change gardens from dull winter brown to bright green. It's spring.

5

Insects buzz and hum from leaf to flower. High in a tree, there is a bird's nest, hidden by green leaves. In the nest are baby birds. The days are long, sunny, and hot.

It is summer.

Leaves turn red, orange, yellow, and brown. The bird's nest is empty now. Dry leaves crunch beneath your feet.

The days are growing short and cool. For the farmers, it is time to harvest crops. It is autumn.

Winter . . . spring . . . summer . . . autumn—these are the four seasons of the year. In most countries, winter and summer are very different. Winter is very cold, and summer is very hot.

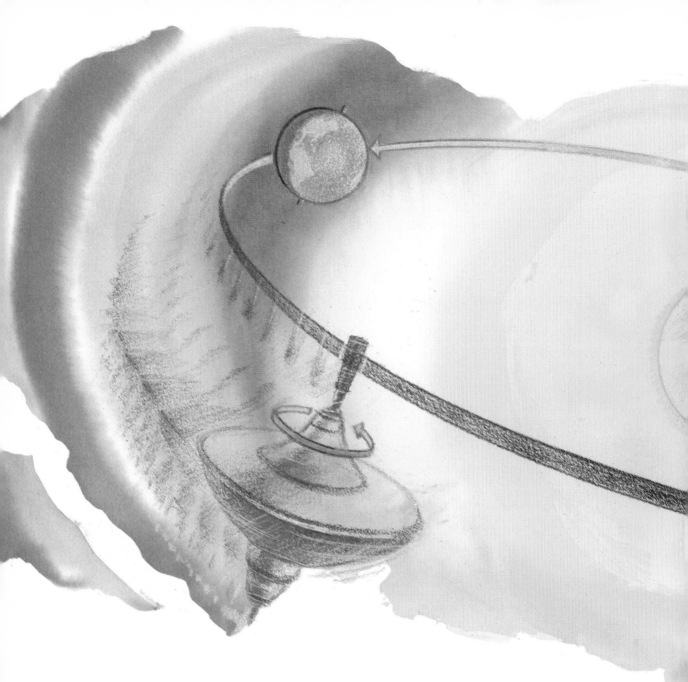

Why do we have seasons? Much of the reason has to do with the movement of the Earth around the sun. The Earth travels around the sun in a circle called an *orbit*. This orbit takes 365 days. The Earth takes one year to make one full orbit of the sun.

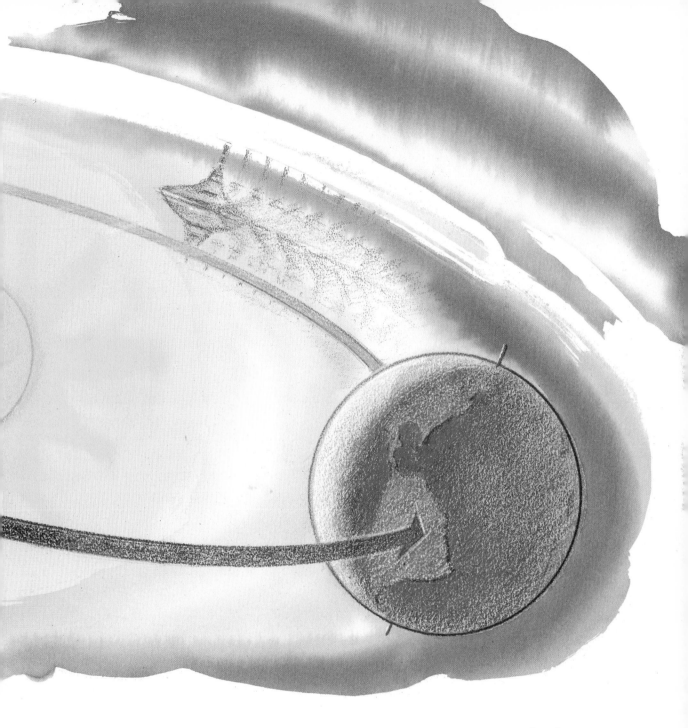

As the Earth makes its journey around the sun, it does
something else. It spins. The Earth is very much like a giant
top that never stops spinning.

Each full spin of the Earth takes 24 hours. For some of those hours, part of the Earth faces the sun. Those hours of light are called day.

The rest of the time, that same part of the Earth faces away from the sun. Those hours of darkness are called night.

If the Earth did not spin, half of it would have day all the time. And the other half would have night all the time. Nothing can live where it is always night. Almost all plants and animals need light and warmth to live.

The Earth leans, or tilts, as it spins and travels around the sun. We have seasons because the Earth spins *and* leans. The part of the Earth leaning toward the sun has summer. The part leaning away from the sun has winter.

Imagine the Earth as a large ball. At the top of the ball is the North Pole. It is not a real pole. It is just a name for the one spot on Earth that is north of every other place.

The North Pole is a cold, icy region, where no plants grow. The polar bears, seals, and birds that live near the North Pole must search very hard to find food.

At the widest part of the Earth between the poles is the *equator*. This imaginary line divides the Earth into two equal parts. Everything between the North Pole and the equator is in the Northern Hemisphere.

Some places near the equator are very wet, because it rains every day. These places are called jungles.

Other places near the equator are very dry, because it seldom rains there. Many of the world's deserts are found in these dry places. But wet or dry, it is always hot near the equator.

At the bottom of the Earth is the South Pole. It is exactly on the other side of the Earth from the North Pole. Here, too, it is always very cold and icy. Penguins and a few other birds live near the South Pole.

But most people, plants, and animals do not live near the poles or on the equator. Instead, they live in other parts of the world, where it is not too cold all the time or too hot all the time.

The way the Earth leans as it spins and travels around the sun affects the seasons in the northern and southern halves of the Earth.

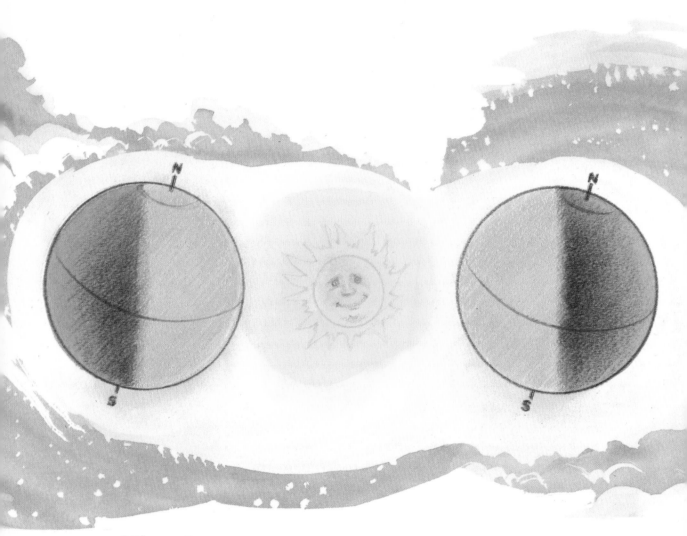

When the North Pole points *toward* the sun, the South Pole points *away* from the sun. That is why when it is summer in the Northern Hemisphere, it is winter in the Southern Hemisphere.

Each year, around June 21, the North Pole leans farthest *toward* the sun. This is the longest day of the year in the northern part of the world. It is the first day of summer.

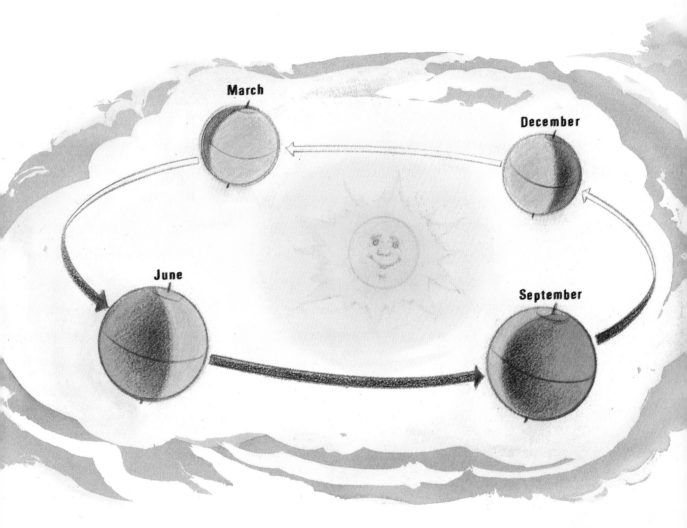

Around September 22, there are exactly 12 hours of day and 12 hours of night all over the world. This is the first day of autumn. After this day, the North Pole will lean away from the sun a little more every day.

Now the days grow shorter in the northern part of the world. Autumn is the season when farmers in the Northern Hemisphere harvest their crops. But it is spring in the southern half of the Earth. There, farmers are planting seeds in their fields.

Every year, around December 21, the North Pole leans farthest away from the sun. This is the shortest day of the year in the Northern Hemisphere. Winter begins on this day.

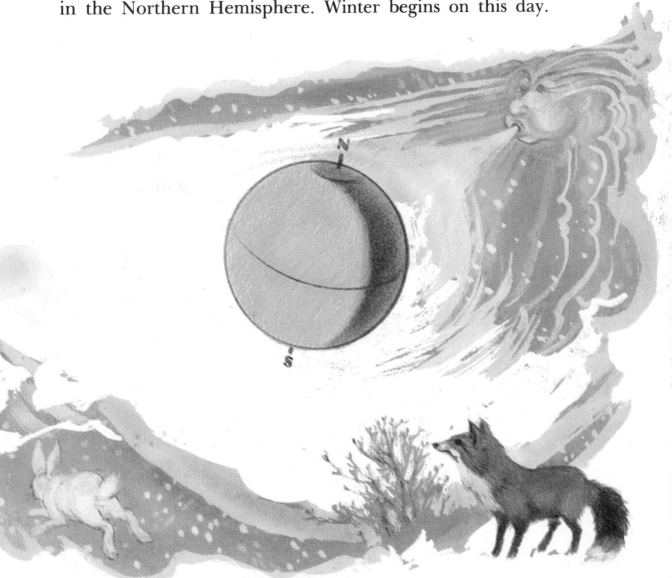

In the winter, the sun is low in the northern sky. The days seem very short, but each day grows a little bit longer as the winter passes.

The first day of spring arrives around March 21. On this day, there are 12 hours of day and 12 hours of night, just as there were on September 22, six months ago. After this day in March, the North Pole again begins to lean toward the sun.

The days grow longer and longer in spring, and the weather grows warmer. Plants begin to turn green. Birds fly back from their warm winter homes. The white winter fur of rabbits turns to brown. Deer and moose begin to grow new antlers. Spring is a season of great change.

But how do the birds know when it is spring, the time to fly north? How do chipmunks know it is time to come out of their burrows in the ground? How do plants know it is time to sprout?

Animals and plants use the sun as a calendar. When it is winter, plants sense that the days are short. Less heat and light reach the Earth.

As spring draws near, Nature's early risers wake up. The crocus and snowdrop bloom early. These flowers do not need many hours of sunlight to make them grow.

Tulips and roses will not bloom until there are more hours of daylight.

Every kind of plant has its own daylight calendar. The magnolia tree flowers long before the apple tree. Some kinds of grass turn green early in the spring. Other kinds do not turn green until June.

Animals follow the same sort of daylight calendar. Robins will return to your garden when there are about 12 hours of daylight. The longer spring days "tell" insects to hatch from their winter shells.

Summer is a warm and wonderful time for life.

All through the year, Nature's creatures pay attention to the daylight calendar. As days grow shorter in August, summer is ending. Trees get ready to drop their leaves. Squirrels begin to store nuts in the ground to eat during cold winter months.

Summer ends, and the school year starts. Autumn brings football, crisp apples, leaves to rake, and pumpkins to carve.

Winter will follow, with snow to shovel and icy ponds to skate upon. But even on the coldest day, spring is drawing closer.

And so the seasons come and go. Nature has made sure that each season brings us an exciting, different world.